YES SHE DID!

MILITARY

Yes She Did! Military

Copyright © 2014
Published by Scobre Educational
Written by Barbara Rudow

Scobre Educational
2255 Calle Clara
La Jolla, CA 92037

Scobre Operations & Administration
42982 Osgood Road
Fremont, CA 94539

www.scobre.com
info@scobre.com

Scobre Educational publications may be purchased for educational, business, or sales promotional use.

Cover and layout design by Jana Ramsay
Copyedited by Susan Sylvia
Some photos by Getty Images

ISBN: 978-161570-877-2 (Soft Cover)
ISBN: 978-1-61570-890-1 (Library Bound)

TABLE OF CONTENTS

CHAPTER 1
DISGUISED...4

CHAPTER 2
BROKEN BARRIERS...11

CHAPTER 3
THE FRONT LINES...20

CHAPTER 4
PERMISSION TO ENGAGE...27

CHAPTER 5
FORWARD, MARCH!...35

CHAPTER 1
DISGUISED

Women have been in the military for over 200 years—just not officially. Most women who helped in the early war efforts, as far back as The Revolutionary War, were known as camp followers. It was their job to follow the men so they could take care of them. The women

HELPING HANDS

Women helped with many jobs, such as loading canons, before they were allowed to officially join the military.

did the cooking, sewing, laundry, and cleaning. They also took care of the sick and wounded. The braver women carried water to the front lines to keep the cannon barrels from overheating. However, some women opted to fight, even though it was not allowed. Many women felt a need to help during the wars but for some, being in the background wasn't enough.

Elizabeth Newcom joined the Army in 1847, during the Mexican-American War. She served in Company D of the Missouri Volunteer Infantry, under the name "Bill Newcom." Back then, they did not ask many questions upon joining; you just had to look the part. Women, like Elizabeth, cut their hair and padded their clothing to disguise their bodies. Elizabeth marched all the way from Missouri to Colorado with her unit (over 600 miles) before they found out she was a girl. As soon as she was discovered, they kicked her out.

Thousands of women braved the consequences of their actions to fight. Just like the men, they too felt the desire to defend their country. And many women still feel that way today.

Though women have fought alongside men for most of our history, they were not officially able to join the military until 1901. Although they no longer had to be disguised, their roles were still limited, and their presence was not always recognized. We have come a long way since the camp followers, but there are many

DID YOU KNOW...

During the Civil War, women were recruited as spies. They were instructed to flirt with enemy soldiers to acquire information.

hurdles yet to conquer. You can tell the military is still a "man's" place when you hear the story of Captain Tammy Duckworth.

Captain Duckworth was a Black Hawk helicopter pilot. In November, 2004, she was serving as a co-pilot in Iraq, just returning from Baghdad. A radio call came in asking her crew to go pick up some American soldiers and bring them home. They picked up the soldiers and were heading back to base when they flew into an unexpected ambush. Captain Duckworth recalls hearing something hit the helicopter, and she knew they were in

LET FREEDOM RING

Many women fought for our freedom. The Liberty Bell in Philadelphia is a symbol of that freedom.

7

trouble. They had been hit by a rocket-propelled grenade. She says her training kicked in and she was so focused on landing the crashing helicopter that she did not realize she had been critically injured. Most helicopters that go down end up on fire with no survivors. Captain Duckworth did not want that to happen

8

to her crew. That was the last thing she remembered.

When Captain Duckworth woke up 10 days later, she was at Walter Reed Memorial Hospital in Washington, D.C. She was happy to learn that, due to her heroic flying efforts, her entire crew survived. However, she was now a double amputee; she had lost both of her legs. She had to remain in the hospital for a long time and as is customary, she was given a "comfort kit" which contained items to help her during her hospital stay. The kit contained a razor, men's slippers, and jockey shorts (men's underwear). Later, Captain Duckworth was able to joke about this experience. "It was great. I don't have feet, so I can't wear the slippers, and you know, I just had my legs blown off, it's not like I'm gonna shave my legs any time soon," she chuckles. The military had not yet made the necessary

DID YOU KNOW...

Tammy hung these words from The Soldier's Creed in her hospital room to help her through her recovery. "I will always place the mission first. I will never quit. I will never accept defeat. I will never leave a fallen comrade."

9

adjustments for women in the military. "They just had kits for men," Duckworth says. "It never occurred to them to make kits for women."

This may be a funny quote, but the reality is that women still continue to fight for equal rights in the military. They do not have all the same opportunities, and some women face discrimination. But for many women, like fighter pilot Major Nicole Malachowski, that does not stop them from realizing their dreams. They work alongside men and they fight hard to break down the barriers.

DID YOU KNOW...

Since her recovery, Tammy Duckworth has run marathons (in a wheelchair), gone snow skiing, and has started flying again. She says this is her second chance in life and she plans to make the most of it.

CHAPTER 2
BROKEN BARRIERS

Nicole was just five years old when she went to an airshow in Nevada. She stared up at the fighter jets zooming past, flying in tight formation, and she knew that one day she was going to be a fighter pilot. Over the years, she excitedly shared her dream with others. Some people encouraged her—but some told her that women couldn't be fighter pilots. Many thought it was too hard, or too dangerous. Nicole didn't listen to them. She took flying lessons in middle school, and joined

CLIMBING HIGHER

Soldiers endure intense physical training to prepare them for the hardships of war.

11

the Civil Air Patrol and the ROTC (Reserve Officer's Training Corps). When she was old enough, she entered the Air Force Academy and her fighter pilot training began.

The training required to become a pilot is long, hard, and competitive. It all starts with Ground School. Candidates must pass tests about the aircrafts and how they work. This means they have to understand some of the most technologically advanced systems in the world. They must also pass physical tests to ensure that they can handle the job. But even if they can handle it, things can, and do, go wrong. To prepare for that, soldiers also go through survival training. Pilots must know how to eject from the helicopter over both land and water, and also how to survive once they do land. If they go down in enemy territory, it's important to know how to avoid being captured. Finally, they must learn how to survive if they are captured and become a prisoner of war.

The controls in the cockpit of this fighter jet show why it is critical for pilots to understand technology.

After all that, they finally start learning to actually fly the aircraft. But that still does not make you a pilot. Many people get this far, only to realize that they do not have the flying skills to be a pilot. Not Nicole. After years of this rigorous training, Nicole finally silenced the skeptics. She became a female fighter pilot!

Being a fighter pilot is exciting, and dangerous. When you watch movies like *Top Gun* you get a glimpse into the life of a fighter pilot. It does have a glamorous side, but it is also dangerous. Pilots must be brave, aggressive, and disciplined. It is an elite group. Only the very top candidates actually make it all the way to the cock-pit. And even though they are the very best, the risks are great. One fighter pilot summed it up this way: "One day you will walk out to your aircraft knowing that it's your last flight in a fighter. Or, one day you will walk out to your aircraft *not* knowing that it is your last flight in a fighter."

Fighter pilots find themselves in extremely dangerous situations on a daily basis, but that doesn't stop them. Major Nicole Malachowski, whose radio call name is "FiFi," has over 1,000 hours in the F-15E Strike Eagle aircraft. She has nearly 200 hours of combat time, including one tour in Iraq (a "tour" is a

FLYING HIGH

Nicole Malachowski (left) poses in front of her F16 with fellow pilot, Samantha Weeks. Major Malachowski blazed the way for female pilots in the Thunderbirds.

designated time in which you are sent to serve, usually in combat). She also served as an instructor and flight commander. She definitely did not let the danger keep her from fulfilling her dream of becoming a great fighter pilot.

And Major Malachowski went one step further. She not only fulfilled her dream, she made history. She was the first female fighter pilot in the entire U.S. military to be selected to fly on a high performance jet team. She became the first female pilot of the Thunderbirds. The Thunderbirds, also known as "The Ambassadors in Blue," perform demonstrations at airshows, just like the one that motivated Nicole to join the military. It is a very competitive position. Only the best pilots are chosen for this team. Nicole was selected to fly the #3 jet as the right wing pilot in the diamond formation. The jets fly in formation at 450-500 mph, and they get as close as 18 inches apart! Flying for the Thunderbirds

THE THUNDERBIRDS

The Air Force Thunderbirds perform at the 2001 Air & Sea show in Ft. Lauderdale, Florida.

was not only an honor for Major Nicole Malachowski, it was also a milestone for women. The day she became the first female Thunderbird, a major barrier for women was knocked down.

Two years later, in 2008, Ann Dunwoody knocked down another barrier for women in the military. When Ann Dunwoody joined the Army, her plan was to serve for two years. She came from a military family (her grandfather, father, and brother were all officers), and although she was just as patriotic, she did not see the Army as a career. However, from the moment she put on the uniform, everything changed. Ann knew that she was exactly where she was supposed to be.

Ann started her military career as a platoon leader. A platoon is the smallest unit in the military. It was a humble beginning but she worked hard and she always looked for opportunities to grow.

While serving as a soldier, she took classes and eventually earned not one, but *two* masters degrees: one in Logistics Management, and one in National Resource Strategy. Ann seemed to be in the right place as each door was opened for women, and she pushed right through. Only a year after the Army promoted its first female soldier to Major General, General Ann Dunwoody was put in command of a mixed-gender company. After that, she continued to climb through the ranks, earning praise

DID YOU KNOW...

General Ann Dunwoody is often found on lists of the most powerful women in the entire world.

GETTING "PINNED"

General Ann Dunwoody receives her rank insignia as a Four-Star General.

and respect along the way. She had many different assignments, including the position of 82nd Division Parachute Officer. During her time with the division, she was called upon to deploy in Desert Shield and Desert Storm. She was also the Commander General in charge of one of the largest departments in the Army. General Dunwoody was in charge of 69,000 employees in all 50 states, and stationed in 145 countries.

General Dunwoody had an impressive career, and earned an extensive list of awards. Eventually she was nominated for the highest rank possible: Four-Star General. Because this position carries the highest responsibilities in the military, candidates must be nominated by the President of the United States (he is the Commander in Chief of the military). Then the candidate must be confirmed by the Senate. General Dunwoody is the first female in the history of our country to achieve this rank. There are approximately 2.7 million people in the military, and General Ann Dunwoody is the only woman who is a Four-Star General!

Women like Major Malachowski, General Dunwoody, and the brave women who fought before them and beside them, have worked hard to advance the position of women in the military. When Dunwoody received her four stars, she said, "I've heard from moms and dads that they see this promotion as a beacon of hope for their own daughters, and as affirmation that anything is possible through hard work and commitment."

But there was still one more hurdle that women were set to clear – direct combat.

CHAPTER 3
THE FRONT LINES

Until 2013, women were not allowed to fight on the front lines but they often ended up there "unofficially." Before January 2013, the policy stated that women weren't allowed in the infantry because they did not want them to directly engage the enemy. The infantry is the unit that fights on foot, face to face, so it usually has the most casualties. There were many soldiers who disagreed with this policy, but until it was changed to include

IN HARM'S WAY

Direct combat on the front lines is extremely dangerous, but the soldiers train hard to be as prepared as possible.

women, they abided by it—
or got around it.

Female soldiers always had the skills necessary at the front lines, but because they were barred from being there, they couldn't be assigned to direct combat. Instead, they were "attached" to a battalion in a position such as a medic, intelligence officer, or military policewoman. That put them near the front lines where they were needed, without actually assigning them to a direct combat position. It sounds like a clever plan, but it got very confusing during the wars in Iraq and Afghanistan. Because there were enemy fighters around nearly every corner, it was hard to tell exactly where the "front lines" started and ended. As a result, many female soldiers ended up in direct combat despite the official policy at that time.

Leigh Ann Hester was a young soldier with the Kentucky's National Guard Police squad. She was sent to Iraq to provide security for a convoy. This included

searching for explosives along the convoy route. There were about 30 vehicles in the convoy that she was protecting.

Without warning, the convoy was attacked by 50 enemy fighters, who were firing grenades and machine guns from irrigation ditches near the road. The enemy fighters also blocked the road, giving the convoy no means of escape. It was a well-orchestrated attack. Sergeant Hester didn't have time to think about where the front lines were; she was in combat. She skillfully maneuvered her team through the "kill zone" to help cut off the attack. Hester and her unit jumped from their Humvees and set up behind a small hill. They fired rifles and grenades. Hester and another soldier attacked three trenches using grenades and M203 grenade-launcher rounds. They killed three enemy fighters, saving the lives of many people in the convoy. The firefight lasted 90 minutes. In the end, only three U.S. soldiers were injured. The U.S. forces killed 27 Iraqis, injured six, and captured one.

Sergeant Hester didn't stop to think about where the front lines were; she did what she had been trained to do. She was a soldier who did her job, and she did it well. For her heroic actions that day, Sergeant Hester was awarded The Silver Star. She is the first woman since World War II to win the Silver Star Medal for valor in combat. Those who disagreed with the old Pentagon policy barring women from combat pointed to Hester as a great example of how women are capable of handling combat situations.

DID YOU KNOW...

The Silver Star is mostly gold! The tiny silver star has golden rays, it is surrounded by a gold wreath, and it sits inside a large gold star.

They also pointed to another hero in combat – Army Medic Specialist (SPC) Monica Lin Brown. Monica Brown is only the second female since WWII to win the Silver Star Medal of valor. Like Sergeant Hester, Brown found herself in combat and reacted with professionalism and courage.

Monica Brown is an Army medic and under the rules of war, medics are not supposed to be shot at while they are doing their job. However, the enemy does not always follow the rules. SPC Brown was in Afghanistan when a hidden bomb ripped through one of the vehicles in her convoy. SPC Brown escaped from her vehicle, but five of her fellow soldiers were in serious trouble. The explosion ignited the fuel tank on their vehicle and turned it into a giant fireball. Miraculously, the five injured soldiers crawled out. But they were immediately under attack by the enemy. Bullets were flying everywhere.

SPC Brown did not stop to worry about where the front lines were. She grabbed her bag and ran to help. Ignoring the danger around her, SPC Brown ran to the men to assess their wounds. In addition to the enemy fire,

COURAGE UNDER FIRE

SPC Brown receives her Silver Star from Vice President Dick Cheney .

the ammunition in their Humvee started to explode, as well. She knew she had to get the injured men to a safer place, and quickly.

She dragged the men a distance of nearly three football fields, using her own body to shield the injured soldiers from the mortar shells (projectile bombs) that were falling around them. Her heroic actions that day saved lives, and for that, SPC Monica Lin Brown became the second woman to receive the Silver Star for valor in combat.

Both Leigh Hester and Monica Lin Brown were forced to respond when fighting broke out around them. They had not been

assigned to the front lines, but they fought anyway. The wars in Afghanistan and Iraq forced many women into combat, and women proved themselves to be not only highly qualified, but also heroic. And now, there are many females in the military who will have the opportunity to fight alongside men on the front lines.

And while some female soldiers are holding their own on the front lines, there are many soldiers that are making their mark in other ways. Beyond serving their country, many female soldiers use their military experience to reach out and help their communities. Soldiers, such as Vernice "Flygirl" Armour, use their training to help people to follow their dreams.

CHAPTER 4
PERMISSION TO ENGAGE

Vernice Armour saw a woman in a flight suit and knew that she would be a pilot someday. What she didn't know, was that she would be the first African American combat pilot in the entire United States Marine Corps.

Being first is not new to Vernice. She was the first African American on the Nashville Police Department's motorcycle squad. She was Camp Pendleton's Female Athlete of the Year, and she won Camp Pendleton's

RAPID RESPONSE

Motorcycle policemen play a key role in law enforcement. The motorcycle allows them to maneuver in crowded streets, which helps them respond to calls more quickly.

Strongest Warrior competition multiple times. As if that wasn't enough, she also graduated number one in her class at flight school. Vernice is competitive, ambitious, and driven; all traits that lead to success.

Vernice went from being a beat cop (foot patrol) to being a combat pilot in just three years. Almost as soon as she earned her wings, she found herself flying the Super Cobra in combat in Iraq. Her orders were to support the ground troops with air cover. On one mission, Captain Armour recalls her fear, not for herself, but for the troops on the ground. And also for the awful possibility of failure.

Captain Vernice "Flygirl" Armour was on a mission in Iraq. She was called to

HELP FROM ABOVE

The Super Cobra is called for when they need firepower from the air. It is an attack helicopter, and it can go 169 mph.

help some troops on the ground who were pinned down with no ammunition left. Their only hope was

help from above. Captain Armour flew in and locked in on the target. She was low on gas and had only one missile on board so she had to get it right or American lives would be lost. She held her breath and pulled the trigger. Nothing happened. With no other options, Captain Armour desperately pulled the trigger again. It worked! For Flygirl, failure—or even being second best—has never been an option. After serving two tours in Iraq, Captain Flygirl Armour chose to affect lives in a different way. She is now an author, consultant, and a highly successful motivational speaker. She uses her combat experience, and military ideas, to help people design "flight plans" for their personal lives.

In the Marines, before pilots can shoot their weapons, they have to get permission to engage the enemy. Vernice Armour now uses that as the basis for her inspiring program. She tells people that they have permission to engage. In other words, she encourages them to take action and work to achieve their goals and dreams. Flygirl has always lived her life by this philosophy. Whether as a successful pilot, or a motivational speaker, she uses her talents to help others.

That is also the path chosen by Coast Guard Lt. Commander Angelina Hidalgo. Angelina Hidalgo was one of the first Hispanic female captains in the United States Coast Guard. At just 24 years old, she was also one of the youngest. It usually takes about ten years of service to become the captain of a vessel, but Hidalgo rose quickly through the ranks to earn the position, as well as the respect of her crew. As captain of the 87-foot Kingfisher patrol boat, Hidalgo was responsible for her entire crew, the $3 million vessel, and the

DID YOU KNOW...

Vernice "Flygirl" Armour wrote a book called Zero to Breakthrough. *She encourages people to step up and be leaders.*

success of each duty they were assigned. One of the Coast Guard's duties is to perform search and rescue missions, such as the one when Hidalgo was asked to respond to a downed plane in the Atlantic Ocean, eight miles off the Florida coast.

A survey plane conducting research on endangered whales crashed into the ocean with four people on board. The Coast Guard was notified, and Hidalgo and the Kingfisher rushed to help. They, along with another vessel, had to search

FULL SPEED AHEAD

This 87-foot Coast Guard Cutter can go 30 knots. It is used for law enforcement and rescue operations.

The Coast Guard helps in many ways. Here they are helping flood victims in New Orleans.

an area covering 300 square miles. The Coast Guard was able to find many items from the plane. They also recovered one body. Eventually, the plane was recovered and the remaining bodies were found, bringing closure for their families.

Although missions like that can be hard, Angelina Hidalgo performs her job with professionalism and sets a great example for others to follow. In addition to captaining the Kingfisher, managing law enforcement, and overseeing many search and rescue operations, Hidalgo also worked as a maritime terrorism analyst.

But that was not enough for Hidalgo. She wanted to do more to help others in her community. Angelina wanted to help kids, so she got involved in the International Trade Education Program (ITEP). Through this program, students from under-privileged or impoverished neigborhoods get a chance

to succeed. Students get academic opportunities and exposure to various career paths. Some also get personal mentoring from caring professionals such as Angelina Hidalgo. A special Coast Guard Day event, organized by Hidalgo, allowed more than 200 ITEP students to visit a base and see firsthand what it is like to serve in the Coast Guard. The event was such a success that it is now an annual gathering.

It is for this type of commitment and service to others, that Angelina Hidalgo received the National Latina Symposium Distinguished Service Award. This award honors Latinas who have shown outstanding dedication and success in their field. But it's not about awards for Angelina Hidalgo—it's about serving others.

In an interview, Hidalgo was asked how the Coast Guard differed from the other military branches, and why she chose it. She answered, "Military service is one of the highest calls of duty that a person can make. While each service is distinct in its missions and in its cultural nuances, being a member of any of the armed services requires a life of selfless and dedicated service. The men and women of these services are all equally humble patriots that ensure that our nation is secure and for me, the Coast Guard's primary and integral mission of search and rescue was appealing. Helping people has always been one of the most important passions in my life."

Armour and Hidalgo both stepped up to be leaders in their communities, choosing to use their experience to help others. Some soldiers, such as Latoya Lucas, step up even when they can no longer be soldiers themselves.

DID YOU KNOW...

There is an elite group in the Coast Guard called the "surfmen." These are the very best boat operators who are called upon in the most extreme conditions. The Surfmen program is comparable to the Navy's "Top Gun" program. But don't let the name fool you – women are surfmen too!

CHAPTER 5
FORWARD, MARCH!

Latoya Lucas grew up in a rough section of Washington, D.C., where gunshots were heard regularly, and drugs were commonplace. Latoya wanted to do something positive with her life so shortly after getting married at age 20, Latoya made a decision. "I recalled hearing stories from my uncle and grandfather about their days in the Army and feeling pride and gratitude for their

PAST AND PRESENT

Washington, D.C., our nation's capital, is known for its rich history, impressive museums, and breathtaking monuments. The Lincoln Memorial is one of the many monuments that draw visitors from around the world.

Iraq is 6,210 miles from Washington, D.C. That is a long way from home when you are fighting for your life!

service," said Latoya. "After months of toying with the idea, I also came to the decision to serve my country." She joined the Army and became Specialist Latoya Lucas. Just one year later, she gave birth to a daughter. Things were going great. She had a family, and a successful Army career. But at age 24, she found herself fighting in Iraq, soon to be fighting for her life.

Latoya was in a convoy, going on an innocent supply run, when a rocket-propelled grenade hit her vehicle, throwing her from the burning wreck. She recalls lying there thinking she was going to die. And she almost did. Along with other serious complications, she had a traumatic brain injury, hearing loss, a fractured pelvis, snapped bones in her hands and arms, and shrapnel injuries. It took her more than two years to recover. She received the Purple Heart (an award given to those who are injured or killed in combat) but she was forced to retire because of the severity of her wounds.

That didn't stop Latoya from serving her country. Latoya now travels the country reminding people that the war doesn't end for soldiers once they end their tour. She says, "It's important for us to be there for our service members when they come back from the battlefield, and we need to be there for them as a nation, as a country when they come back because they are going to come back with issues." Latoya could no longer serve in the military, but she could still serve the military by helping in this way. She was a successful soldier, and now she is a successful public speaker. Her work is smoothing the way for soldiers everywhere.

DID YOU KNOW...

One out of every four veterans in the wars in Iraq and Afghanistan will end up with service related disabilities. That is over 633,000 disabled veterans so far – and the wars are not over yet.

DID YOU KNOW...

In January 2013, the Pentagon lifted its ban on women in many combat positions. There are still some restrictions, but the military is finally marching in the right direction.

Like Latoya, Tammy Duckworth, also a Purple Heart recipient, served the military after her injuries prevented her from being a soldier. She was appointed by Barack Obama as the assistant secretary of Veteran Affairs. She worked tirelessly to protect and improve the standard of care for military veterans. She helped in areas of health care, mental health, housing, employment, and homelessness. She also helped with a major reorganization of the system so that veterans could get the help they needed after they selflessly served our country.

Tammy Duckworth then took another step, another first for women. She became the first Asian-American Congresswoman in Illinois. Standing tall and proud on prosthetic legs, Tammy was also recognized as the first combat-injured female member of congress in the history of the United States.

These women, plus individuals like Vernice Armour, Angelica Hidalgo, Nicole Malachowski, Leigh Hester, and Monica Lin Brown, have blazed the way for women every-where. They are leaders for the United States of America. They

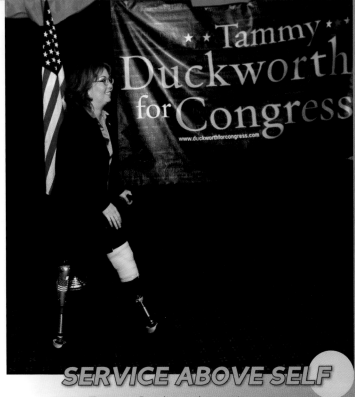

SERVICE ABOVE SELF

Tammy Duckworth continues to serve the people of our country by serving in the United States congress.

love to serve. As Nicole Malachowski states, "Women love their country too, and there are a lot of us who choose to do that by wearing a military uniform. I have seen and traveled the world, and it is just a wonderful thing to be a woman living in a country that provides you so many wonderful opportunities and freedoms that are unmatched anywhere else in the world."

PROUD TO SERVE

"I pledge allegiance to the Flag of the United States of America, and to the Republic for which it stands, one nation under God, indivisible, with liberty and justice for all."

The military offers unique challenges for women, but thanks to the women featured in this book, it is definitely evolving. Women are marching forward. And so can you. As Flygirl says, "Don't let anyone dash your hopes and dreams. Decide what and where you want to be and take positive steps to get there." No matter what you do in life, remember the Army slogan: "Be all that you can be."